BIOGRAPHY FROM
ANCIENT CIVILIZATIONS
LEGENDS, FOLKLORE, AND STORIES OF ANCIENT WORLDS

The Life and Times of

PERICLES

Mitchell Lane
PUBLISHERS

P.O. Box 196
Hockessin, Delaware 19707

BIOGRAPHY FROM

ANCIENT CIVILIZATIONS

LEGENDS, FOLKLORE, AND STORIES OF ANCIENT WORLDS

Titles
in the Series

The Life and Times of:

Alexander the Great
Archimedes
Augustus Caesar
Buddha
Catherine the Great
Charlemagne
Cleopatra
Confucius
Constantine
Genghis Khan
Hammurabi
Homer
Joan of Arc
Julius Caesar
Marco Polo
Moses
Nero
Pericles
Rameses the Great
Socrates

The Life and Times of

PERICLES

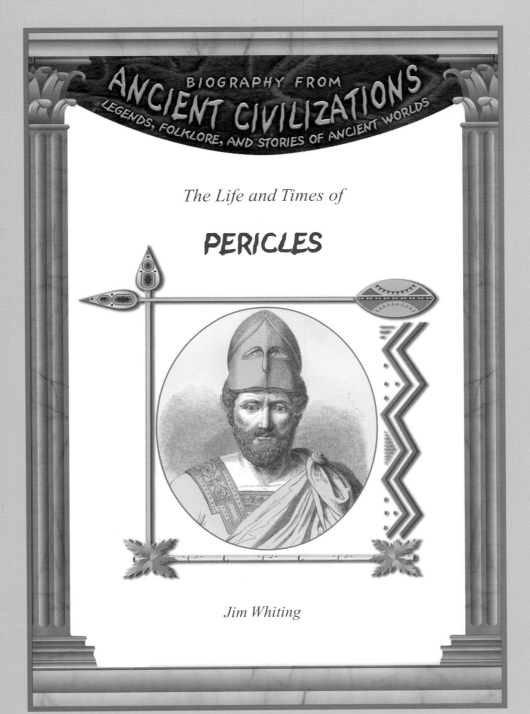

Jim Whiting

Printing   1   2   3   4   5   6   7   8
Library of Congress Cataloging-in-Publication Data

Whiting, Jim, 1943–
    The life and times of Pericles / by Jim Whiting.
        p. cm. — (Biography from ancient civilizations)
    Includes bibliographical references and index.
    ISBN 1-58415-339-3 (library bound)
    1. Pericles, 449–429 B.C.—Juvenile literature. 2. Greece—History—Athenian supremacy, 479–431 B.C.—Juvenile literature. 3. Athens (Greece)—Politics and government—Juvenile literature. 4. Statesmen—Greece—Athens—Biography—Juvenile literature. 5. Orators—Greece—Athens—Biography—Juvenile literature. I. Title. II. Series.
DF228.P4W47 2005
938'.04'092—dc22

                                                                            2004024604

ABOUT THE AUTHOR: Jim Whiting has been a journalist, writer, editor, and photographer for more than 20 years. In addition to a lengthy stint as publisher of *Northwest Runner* magazine, Mr. Whiting has contributed articles to the *Seattle Times*, *Conde Nast Traveler*, *Newsday*, and *Saturday Evening Post*. He has edited more than 100 Mitchell Lane titles in several series. A great lover of classical music and history, he has written many books for young adults, including *The Life and Times of Irving Berlin* and *The Life and Times of Julius Caesar* (Mitchell Lane). He lives in Washington state with his wife and two teenage sons.

PHOTO CREDITS: Cover, pp. 1, 3—Archive Photos/Getty Images; p. 6—Jamie Kondrchek; p. 9—Hellenic Ministry of Culture; p. 11—World Maps; pp. 12, 40—Bettman/Corbis; p. 14—Livius; p. 18—Superstock; p. 20—Yasou; p. 22—SNC; p. 30—Time Life Pictures/Mansell/Getty Images; p. 33—Birmingham Museum and Art Gallery; p. 34—Hulton Archive/Getty Images; p. 36—insecula.

PUBLISHER'S NOTE: This story is based on the author's extensive research, which he believes to be accurate. Documentation of such research is contained on page 47.

The internet sites referenced herein were active as of the publication date. Due to the fleeting nature of some web sites, we cannot guarantee they will all be active when you are reading this book.

BIOGRAPHY FROM

ANCIENT CIVILIZATIONS

LEGENDS, FOLKLORE, AND STORIES OF ANCIENT WORLDS

The Life and Times of

PERICLES

Chapter 1   Winning Against All Odds 7
             FYInfo*: The Marathon
                 Run 13
Chapter 2   A Rising Star 15
             FYInfo: The Origins of
                 Drama 21
Chapter 3   Building for the Ages 23
             FYInfo: The Acropolis 29
Chapter 4   Love and War 31
             FYInfo: Spartan Warfare 35
Chapter 5   The Greek Tragedy 37
             FYInfo: English Words from
                 Greek 42
Chronology 43
Timeline in History 44
Chapter Notes 45
Glossary 46
For Further Reading 47
             Works Consulted 47
             On the Internet 47
Index 48

*For Your Information

Xerxes became ruler of the Persian Empire in 486 B.C. He continued preparations for the invasion of Greece his father had begun. Despite raising a huge army and navy, he was defeated.

CHAPTER
ONE

WINNING AGAINST ALL ODDS

On a hot summer morning, a small Athenian army looked out anxiously from their hillside camp across the plain of Marathon. Less than nine thousand strong, they saw what seemed to be a sea of Persian warriors. In 490 B.C., Persia was the world's leading superpower, ruling a vast empire that stretched in an unbroken swath from modern India to Turkey. For several generations, Persian soldiers had acquired a reputation for invincibility. Sometimes their opponents would surrender without a fight. Their ferocity was the main reason the Persian Empire had steadily expanded.

Now it was the Athenians' turn—even though they occupied a puny territory encompassing just a few hundred square miles. A few years earlier, Athens—one of hundreds of tiny city-states that dotted the map of Greece—had supported a brief rebellion by the Greek settlement of Miletus (see map on p. 11), which lay on the west coast of modern-day Turkey. The rebellion had been ruthlessly crushed. The Persians decided to punish the Athenians for helping to support it. They sent hundreds of ships and an estimated 30,000 men to capture the city. This formidable force splashed ashore in the expansive Bay of Marathon.

The Athenians, forewarned of the Persian landing, sent their entire army to Marathon and arrived in time to control the one road that led to Athens, about 20 miles away. The two sides faced each other for more than a week without taking any action. The Athenians had hoped that the Spartans—another city-state famous for the high quality of its warriors—would join them in this crucial fight. But a day or two earlier, a long-distance runner named Pheidippides (pronounced fie-DIP-uh-deez) had returned from Sparta with chilling news. The Spartans were in the midst of a religious ritual. They would come when it was over, in about a week.

On this morning, the Athenians didn't have a week. They didn't even have a few hours. Athenian lookouts spotted part of the enemy force reboarding their ships. The tactic was obvious. Marathon was on one side of a peninsula. The city of Athens was on the other side. The bulk of the Persian army would remain at Marathon to tie down the Athenians. The troops now clambering onto the ships would sail around the tip of the peninsula, head up the other side, and easily capture the undefended city.

The Athenian generals held a brief conference. They had already decided how they would fight the battle. Now it was time to put their plan into action. They passed their orders to the troops. The men were not professional soldiers. Nearly all of them owned small farms in the countryside outside Athens or operated small businesses inside the city. They had to purchase their own army equipment. Now it was time to use it.

Grimly, the men began fastening bronze shinguards called greaves onto their lower legs. Bronze corselets protected their chest, stomach, and back. Heavy bronze helmets sported horsehair crests that seemed to add another foot to their height. Then they grabbed their *hoplons*—thick, round wooden shields three feet in diameter—and their long wooden spears tipped with deadly iron points. They must have been perspiring heavily. Temperatures were already well into the 80s, and their equipment weighed over 50 pounds.

These are bronze greaves. Athenian soldiers strapped them onto the front of their shins. They provided protection for the soldiers' lower legs against sword thrusts.

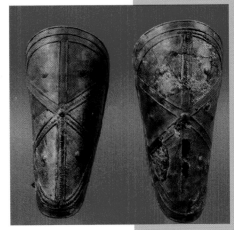

After forming their units, they came down off the hill and began marching toward the Persian lines, about a mile away. As they drew closer, Persian archers launched arrows at them. The Athenians raised their shields. Nearly all of the missiles bounced harmlessly away. Singing their battle song, the Athenians readied their spears and began jogging toward the enemy.

While the advancing Athenians may have seemed like an unbroken line to the waiting Persians, that wasn't quite the case. They were divided into three sections, and those sections were not of equal strength. As the Persians soon discovered, the center consisted of just over a thousand men. Even though they weren't as heavily armed as their attackers, the Persians opposite the Athenian center absorbed the initial charge and began pushing the Athenians back. Their generals must have smiled as they anticipated yet another military success.

If they did, they gloated too soon. The weakness in the Athenian center masked the Athenian strategy, which was to build up the strength of their two wings. These heavily reinforced wings hacked their way through their enemies. Then they wheeled and rushed to the aid of their embattled comrades in the center.

The Persians were trapped. With thousands of heavily armed men bearing down on them, they panicked. Many threw away their weapons and tried to run away, seeking the safety of their ships. Only then did they make a stand. Several prominent Athenians were killed on the beaches as the frightened Persians finally made their escape. They left behind the corpses of more than 6,000 of their comrades. According to contemporary sources, just 192 Athenians died.

But the danger hadn't passed. The Persian ships began rowing rapidly to the south. Their intention was obvious—to catch up with the ships that had left earlier. They could still capture Athens. The battle-weary Athenian soldiers—a number of them suffering from wounds—cut their rejoicing short. They had to get back home before their enemies arrived. They set off in a desperate race.

The Athenians won. When the Persian ships arrived, they found the victorious army waiting for them. After a period of indecision, the Persians began the long voyage home. They would be back.

According to legend, Darius the Great, the Persian ruler, ordered one of his slaves to remind him about the Athenians every day. His death in 486 didn't end the threat. His son Xerxes (ZERK-seez) succeeded him and a few years later began raising a huge army of several hundred thousand men and a fleet of hundreds of ships. This time, though, the Spartans were ready to lend a hand. Three hundred of them held off the entire Persian army for three days at the narrow pass of Thermopylae (ther-MAH-puh-lee) until a man who showed the Persians a secret path to their rear betrayed them. Every Spartan perished.

As the Persian juggernaut poured into the countryside outside Athens, the citizens fled to the nearby island of Salamis (SAH-lih-miss). They watched in anger and horror as the Persians burned their city and farms. But an Athenian general named Themistocles (theh-MISS-tuh-kleez) came up with a brilliant plan. He sent a slave to tell the Persians that the Greeks were going to evacuate Salamis the following day. The man told the Persians that they could catch the

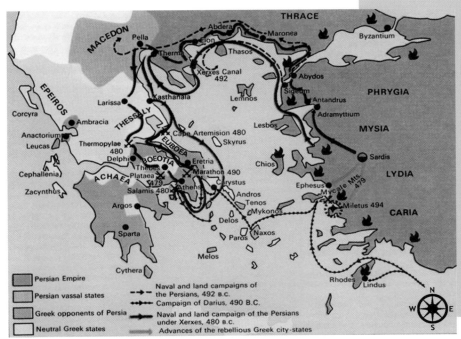

This map shows the locations of the major battles during the two Persian invasions. The first one ended at Marathon in 490 B.C. The second and much larger invasion overwhelmed much of Greece ten years later before being checked at Salamis. Most of the Persians were forced to retreat. The remaining Persian troops were defeated by a combined Athenian and Spartan army the following spring.

fleeing Greeks if they sent their ships into the narrow strait that separates Salamis from the mainland.

Xerxes took the bait. Anticipating an overwhelming victory, he set up an improvised throne on a ridge that overlooks the strait. He watched his navy blunder into a trap. The Persian ships outnumbered the Greeks by more than three to one, but they were forced into a narrow column as they entered the strait. The agile Greek ships swarmed around the leading Persian ships and halted them. As more Persian vessels continued to pour into the bottleneck, the fleet

DARIVS.

Darius the Great was a Persian emperor who ruled from 522 B.C. until his death in 486 B.C. During his reign, the Persian territory reached its furthest extent. He was shocked when his soldiers were defeated at the Battle of Marathon and vowed vengeance. He began preparations to send a much larger army but died before his plans were complete.

became increasingly confined and unable to move. At least two hundred Persian ships were sunk. More were captured. The victory gave the Athenians control of the sea and threatened Persian supply lines. That forced Xerxes and most of his army to pack up and go home. Enough stayed for a battle the following year near the city of Plataea (pleh-TEE-uh). For a while the outcome was in doubt, but the Greeks were ultimately victorious. The Persian threat was over.

What is perhaps the greatest half-century in human history was about to begin. It is unrivaled in terms of its accomplishments in art, architecture, literature, and drama. Above all, it firmly established the democratic principles under which Athens was governed. No one would be more influential in shaping this exciting era than a man who had been a toddler at the time of Marathon and had just entered his teens as the defeated Persians headed home for the final time.

His name is Pericles (PAIR-ih-kleez), and his name is forever connected with what succeeding generations would call the Golden Age of Greece.

The Marathon Run

According to legend, a messenger ran from the battlefield at Marathon to the anxiously awaiting citizens in Athens. He gasped, "Rejoice! We conquer!" and died moments later. When European aristocrats began planning the modern Olympics in Athens in 1896, one of them suggested a footrace that would commemorate this legendary event. Appropriately, the winner of the race, which measured about 21 miles, was a Greek shepherd named Spiridon Louis.

Some of the American participants in those Olympics lived in Boston and decided to establish a similar event in their hometown. The first Boston Marathon was held in 1897 and, except for 1918—when a relay to raise money for American involvement in World War I was substituted—it has been held every year since then. Hundreds of marathons are held worldwide as well. And of course the marathon is one of the most widely watched events during the Olympics.

For the first several years of the marathon, there was no standard distance. At the 1908 Olympics, held in London, England, the Queen Mother asked race officials to change the course they had already laid out—adding more than a mile—so that her grandchildren could watch the start. The resulting course of 26 miles, 385 yards was established as the event's official distance several years later.

According to legend, Pheidippides collapses upon reaching Athens

It is very unlikely that the legend of the messenger is true. The first time it was even mentioned was nearly 500 years after the battle. The contemporary historian Herodotus wrote about a messenger named Pheidippides, who left Athens one morning and arrived in Sparta the following evening—a distance of more than 150 miles—with an urgent message seeking Spartan support for the upcoming battle. Then he ran back with the negative response. Pheidippides and similar messengers were trained to cover such distances easily and efficiently, long before the days of athletic training shoes. It seems doubtful that the relatively short distance of 20 miles, even in the heat of a Greek summer, would have presented any problems to a fit messenger. After all, the entire Athenian army covered the same distance on the same day.

Pericles was very self-conscious about the shape of his head, so he only allowed himself to be portrayed while wearing his helmet.

CHAPTER
TWO

A RISING STAR

Historians know very little about the early years of Pericles. He was probably born in 493 B.C. He had two siblings, an older brother named Ariphron and a younger sister. As was typical in ancient Greece, considering the country's attitudes toward women, no one recorded his sister's name.

Because his mother was a member of one of the city's most famous families, the Alcmaeonids (alk-MEE-on-ids), her name was recorded. It was Agariste (ah-guh-RIS-tee). Her uncle Cleisthenes (KLISE-then-eez) is generally regarded as the founder of the city's democracy. Even though he was an aristocrat himself, he was popular among ordinary Athenians and led a successful revolt against the ruling aristocrats in 507. At that point, he made a startling change in the way that Athens was governed: Every Athenian citizen could vote for the city's leaders. While the new system did not include everyone—women, slaves, and foreigners could not vote—and left some power to the conservative aristocrats, it was the world's first democracy.

Whatever the new system's shortcomings, it was something of which the Athenians were very proud. It may have been one of the major reasons for the victory at Marathon. The Athenians were fighting for what they believed in, while many of the invading Persians had been forced into serving in the army. According to some reports, the Persians were driven forward by officers who whipped them if they showed any hesitation.

As contemporary historian Herodotus (heh-RODD-uh-tuss) noted, the success of the Athenians at Marathon "proved, if proof is needed, how noble a thing equality before the law is, for while they [the Athenians] were oppressed under tyrants, they had no better success in war than any of their neighbors, yet, once the yoke was flung off, they proved the finest fighters in the world."[1]

Pericles' father, Xanthippus (zan-THIH-pus), was a famous general. It is almost certain that he fought at Marathon, which would have given him a great deal of prestige among his fellow citizens. Unfortunately, the enormous civic pride that followed the battle soon wore off. In spite of the glorious victory, different factions in Athens began quarreling with each other. There was a rumor that some of the Alcmaeonids supported the Persians and had flashed signals to them. The family responded by attacking Miltiades (mill-TIE-ah-deez), the greatest hero at Marathon. Not long after the battle, Miltiades proposed an attack on the Greek island of Paros and was appointed as the leader. The invasion went badly and Miltiades was seriously wounded. Xanthippus led the effort to punish his failure with a heavy fine. Miltiades soon died and his son Cimon (KIE-mon) had to pay it.

Eventually it was Xanthippus's turn to suffer. In 484 he fell victim to one of the city's new laws, called ostracism, which allowed the citizens to put limits on the amount of power that anyone could gain. Every year, the Athenian assembly would vote on whether or not someone should be expelled from the city. If a majority voted in favor, a public vote would be held two months later to decide who that person would be. Every citizen had the right to scrawl someone's name on a shard of pottery. The "winner," the one who received the most votes, would be exiled from Athens for ten years. Today, visitors to

Athenian museums can see some of these ancient shards and read the names inscribed on them.

Presumably taking his family with him, Xanthippus left Athens following his ostracism. His banishment didn't last the full ten years, however. With the Persian invasion looming on the horizon, he was asked to return in 480. He became a hero during the war, leading Athenian forces in two battles that helped to defeat the Persians.

It is likely that he left his wife and children behind when he went off to fight. Like nearly everyone in Athens, they must have gone to the island of Salamis to escape the invaders. These experiences would have given young Pericles a taste of the horrors of war and of the fickle nature of the Athenian public. He would acquire a much fuller understanding of both during the rest of his life.

Few Athenians could boast a more impressive set of parents than Pericles. In a sense, Pericles was born with a silver spoon in his mouth. On the other hand, Athenian politics were filled with jealous rivalries. There were no guarantees of success.

One thing that helped him in his future career was an exceptional education. While he was growing up, Pericles would have received the typical education of most well-to-do young Athenians. That included learning how to read and write by using a stylus on a wax tablet. Learning by heart the epic poems of Homer—*The Iliad* and *The Odyssey*—was important. So was music. Pericles probably knew how to play the lyre and the flute, as well as sing. For Athenians, education went beyond developing mental ability. Boys underwent rigorous physical training, which included running and jumping, boxing and wrestling, in addition to other sports.

Because Pericles demonstrated that he was unusually gifted, he received additional instruction from two of the most eminent teachers of his day, Damon and Anaxagoras (an-ak-SAG-or-us). While Damon

The blind poet Homer wrote two epics, The Iliad *and* The Odyssey. *Studying Homer was one of the most important parts of the education of young Athenians. They were required to learn large portions of the two poems.*

was officially a music teacher, he included political theory in his instruction. Even more important was the influence of Anaxagoras, who was among the first "scientific philosophers." He sought natural explanations for events, rather than suggesting that what happened was the will of the gods. He also instructed Pericles in the art of public speaking. In an era without mass media, the best way for politicians to get people to follow them was to be a persuasive speaker.

Author Donald Kagan notes, "Pericles' aristocratic heritage, the influence wielded by the Alcmaeonid side of his family, and the glory of his father's achievements gave him a start in Athenian political life that few could match. The young man who was about to enter Athenian public life was much more than the scion of two noble families. Like other aristocrats, he sought the victory, recognition, and glory that came with political success. Unlike the others, however, he brought to the battle unconventional ideas of greatness for his city and of the possibilities for political leadership."[2]

He began to emerge from the shadows of history in 472 B.C. By that time, plays had become very important in Athenian life. Every year a competition was held in honor of the god Dionysus. The city's leading playwrights would submit their latest work for performance. The citizens would attend all the plays, and then vote for their favorite. Pericles served as *choregos*, or sponsor, of one of those playwrights, a man named Aeschylus (ESS-kuh-luss).

For this competition, Aeschylus departed from the usual custom, which was to write about mythological subjects or events that had happened long ago. His play was *The Persians*, which dealt with the very recent battle of Salamis. Even more unusual, he wrote from the Persian point of view. In spite of its unique approach, *The Persians* won first prize. As Aeschylus's sponsor, Pericles claimed a share of the glory. He may have claimed something else. Themistocles had been more responsible than anyone else for the victory at Salamis. He had convinced the Athenians to use the unexpected discovery of silver not far from the city in 483 to build a large fleet of warships. Those ships were not only the key element for the victory at Salamis three years later, but also for the later development of Athens as a naval power. It is possible that sponsoring this play—which demonstrated the importance of a strong navy—was an early statement of one of the cornerstones of Pericles' political beliefs.

The historical record returns to silence for nearly a decade. Pericles probably got married toward the end of this period, perhaps in 463. The custom of the times was for men to wait until their late twenties or even early thirties to marry. Typically their brides would be in their mid-teens. Just as typically, the names of their brides were hardly ever recorded. That was the case with Pericles, as the name of his wife is unknown. Soon they had two sons, Xanthippus and Paralus (PAR-ah-luss). By Athenian standards, Pericles' marriage was a

The theater of Dionysus was one of the focal points of ancient Athens. Thousands of Athenian citizens happily spent hours sitting on hard stone seats in the hot sun as they watched plays.

success. He had two male heirs to carry on the family name. By today's standards, his marriage was a failure. It ended in divorce. Pericles didn't seem to be particularly upset when he broke up with his wife. He even helped her remarry—her betrothed was one of the wealthiest men in Athens.

His relationship with his sons wasn't very good. Almost nothing is known of Paralus, the younger son. The elder son, Xanthippus, married a rich woman who had even richer tastes. Pericles, who was not very wealthy, gave him a limited allowance. Because he needed more money, Xanthippus went to a rich Athenian and told the man that he needed the money for his father. The lie was exposed when the man came to Pericles and asked to be repaid. Pericles refused and took his son to court. The two of them were never reconciled. Xanthippus began spreading vicious stories about his father.

While Pericles' family life may have been a failure, his public life was among the greatest in history.

The Origins of Drama

For many years before the time of Pericles, Greek religious festivals had included a chorus, a group of singers and dancers who performed the rituals. According to tradition, in about 535 B.C. a man named Thespis set himself apart from the chorus and engaged its members in dialogue. His name lives on in the word *thespian*, which is a synonym for *actor*.

This new form became known as tragedy, which literally means "goat-song." There are several theories about the name. One is that the religious festivals from which they sprang included sacrificing a goat. Another is that the participants wore goatskins. The areas where these tragedies were performed became known as theaters, from a Greek word that means "to look at."

And there was plenty to look at. The ruling aristocrats of the city soon organized formal dramatic contests in honor of Dionysus, the god of wine, revelry, and just plain fun. The theater of Dionysus—its ruins are a popular tourist attraction in Athens—was an outdoor amphitheater that seated thousand of spectators. They sat on hard stone benches for hours on end.

Aeschylus introduced an innovation: a second actor. This allowed interaction between individual characters as well as back-and-forth dialogue between the actors and the chorus. Not long afterward, Sophocles (SOF-uh-kleez) included a third actor, creating even more dramatic possibilities. These two men, along with Euripides (yuh-RIP-eh-deez), are considered the three greatest Greek playwrights. Among them they wrote more than 300 plays. Only 32 survive.

Eventually comedies joined tragedies in Athenian theaters. No one was spared the sharp wit of comic playwrights. They were often merciless in insulting public figures, who had to sit in the front row and listen to their fellow citizens laugh at their onstage portrayals. Many comedies included dialogue that we would consider X-rated.

All the actors were males. They wore masks that not only identified the characters they were playing but also indicated their moods, happy or sad. Sometimes the actors would even take on the roles of gods and goddesses. Utilizing what were probably the world's first special effects, they would "fly" onto the stage with the help of a crane.

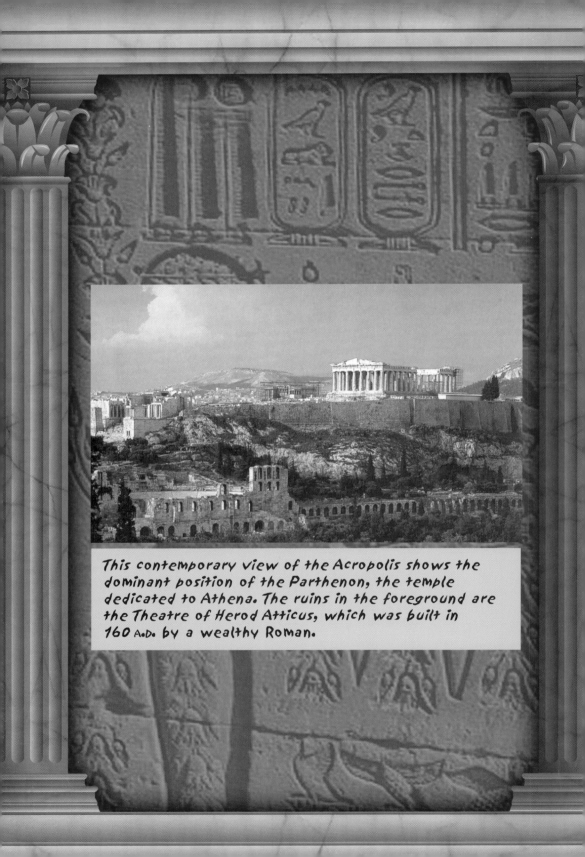

This contemporary view of the Acropolis shows the dominant position of the Parthenon, the temple dedicated to Athena. The ruins in the foreground are the Theatre of Herod Atticus, which was built in 160 A.D. by a wealthy Roman.

CHAPTER
THREE

BUILDING FOR THE AGES

At about the time he was married, Pericles began his political career. Athens did not have organized political parties such as the Democrats and Republicans. Rather, certain prominent individuals gathered groups of supporters around them. As Pericles was doing his political apprenticeship, the dominant politician was Cimon—the son of Miltiades, with whom Pericles' father had feuded. It was customary for families to retain such feuds from one generation to the next. Pericles knew his political advancement would be blocked as long as Cimon was in power.

Athenian politics also reflected the city's relationship with Sparta, the other dominant Greek city-state. Even though the two had combined to defeat Persia, it didn't take long after the victory at Plataea for the fragile alliance to begin crumbling. The Athenians wanted to rebuild the walls around their burned city. The Spartans objected, saying that with the Persians gone, there was no need for defensive walls. Besides, they added, it would show disrespect to them. The Athenians deceived the Spartans until the walls were back up. It was the beginning of nearly half a century of mutual distrust that eventually led to one of history's most tragic wars, a war that would rip Greece apart.

Though the Persians were no longer threatening to invade the Greek mainland, they were still active in the region. To counter Persian influence, the Athenians helped found the Delian League in 478. It was a union of all the Greek city-states and islands that depended on maritime commerce. With its fleet of 200 ships, the Athenians were the centerpiece. The name of the alliance came from the sacred island of Delos, which served as the site of the organization's treasury.

At first, the league proved its value as its warships defeated Persians in several encounters. But the power of Athens soon became so great that the other members became alarmed. In 471, the island of Naxos wanted to withdraw from the league. The Athenians punished them. Six years later, the island of Thásos tried to do the same thing. The Athenians not only invaded but also tore down the city's walls and took it over following a lengthy siege.

These developments caused increasing uneasiness in Sparta, which had virtually no navy at all. Sparta's power was based on its disciplined soldiers.

This uneasiness increased as the Spartans began encountering some internal difficulties: a destructive earthquake and an uprising by its slaves. Spartan soldiers suppressed the revolt, but many slaves escaped and took refuge in the nearby mountains. While no one could stand up to the Spartans in open warfare, their soldiers had trouble trying to capture the rebellious slaves in areas where it was difficult to maneuver. In 462, they appealed to Athens for help, since the Athenians had more experience in that type of fighting.

That appeal set off a furious debate in Athens. Cimon was a friend of Sparta and wanted to lead an army to help them. Ephialtes (ef-ee-ALL-tees)—Cimon's primary rival and the leader of the faction to which Pericles belonged—opposed him. Greek historian Plutarch (PLOO-tark) explains that Ephialtes told his fellow citizens, "They ought not to raise up or assist a city that was a rival to Athens; but that being down, it were best to keep her so, and let the pride and arrogance of Sparta be trodden under."[1]

As Donald Kagan notes, "Cimon and his policies, however, were still popular, and he made an effective reply to the opposition, urging the Athenians 'not to leave Greece lame nor see their city deprived of its yokefellow.' It was a homely but powerful metaphor, comparing Athens and Sparta to a team of oxen pulling the Greek plow, and it strongly appealed to an assembly made up of farmers. It also appealed to warm memories of cooperation in the common cause against the Persians and to the Panhellenic [overall Greek] spirit of that time."[2]

Cimon's argument carried the day, and he set off with several thousand men. Surprisingly, he was back much sooner than anyone had expected. Like oil and water, Athenian democracy and Spartan authoritarianism did not mix. The Spartans asked their guests to leave soon after their arrival, even though the revolt had not been crushed.

Most of the men who had left with Cimon were—like him—conservatives. Even with the liberal democratic reforms that had been instituted several decades earlier, the conservatives had retained considerable power. Ephialtes took advantage of their absence to pass laws that stripped away that power. Cimon tried to undo the damage when he returned. He was too late. The rude, humiliating treatment by the Spartans undermined his prestige. It wasn't surprising that he was ostracized in 461.

What was surprising was that Ephialtes was assassinated about the same time. Political murders in the history of Athenian democracy were rare, as the city normally settled disagreements without violence. Ephialtes' death opened the door for Pericles to come to power.

"We are not told how and why Pericles became head of the faction led by the fallen Ephialtes, but he was well prepared by family tradition and associations, by his unusual education, and by his native abilities to lead the movement toward a fuller democracy and a greater Athens,"[3] Kagan writes. One factor that helped his rise was his election as general. Ten generals were elected every year. In theory, all were equal. In practice, a few—or in Pericles' case, just one— exercised a dominant role.

He built upon the foundation that Ephialtes had established, giving more and more power to all Athenian citizens. One of his most important reforms was sponsoring a law that paid citizens for the time that they served on juries. This was a very important function in Athens, because jurors often spent more than half a year hearing cases that ranged from small private lawsuits to burning questions involving public safety. Providing compensation for time away from work enabled virtually everyone to participate in this important civic function.

We don't know when most of the changes that Pericles advocated took place. The one definite date is 451, when the city enacted a law that withheld Athenian citizenship from children of an Athenian father and a foreign-born mother. The law's primary purpose was to prevent wealthy Athenians from increasing their power by marrying women from aristocratic families in other city-states. Pericles had no way of knowing that this law would come back to haunt him a few years later.

At least as important as his involvement in domestic affairs was his foreign policy. As Cimon's misadventure in Sparta had shown, relations between the two city-states were tense. Cimon's ostracism was probably one reason these tensions flared up in 460. The two sides fought for fifteen years, though many of the battles involved only their respective allies.

At about the same time, the Athenians sent a large force to Egypt, helping to support a rebellion against the ruling Persians. In 454 the Persians won a major victory, nearly wiping out the Athenians. One consequence was that Pericles moved the treasury of the Delian League from Delos to Athens. While the stated reason was to insure that the money would be much safer in Athens than in its exposed location on a tiny island, it demonstrated that what was originally a group of equals was now essentially an empire based in Athens.

Money, supposedly for the common defense of the members, was now entirely under Athenian control.

Under Pericles' direction, Athenian political debates normally dealt with the most pressing issues facing the city. These included religion, maintaining the city's safety (Athens seemed to be almost continually at war with someone), and maintaining its food supply. With a population of 300,000 people, Athens had to import many of its provisions, especially grain for the bread that was a dietary staple. He would construct a monument that reflected the prestige of his city, something that would amaze anyone who saw it. He envisioned a temple and several additional buildings on the Acropolis, the highest point in Athens. The temple, called the Parthenon, would honor Athena, the city's patron goddess.

As noted historian Paul Cartledge writes, "From time to time, however, the occasion arose for making decisions on matters other than the narrowly pragmatic or utilitarian. One such occasion, the chance not just of a lifetime but of an epoch, came in about 450, and Pericles was brilliantly positioned to exploit it."[4]

Pericles had just concluded a mostly favorable settlement with the Persians, which finally ended thirty years of off-and-on combat following their expulsion from Greece. At the same time, the city's treasury was bulging with money. Pericles thought he knew the ideal way of spending it.

The Acropolis had lain almost untouched since being torched by the Persians several decades earlier. Many citizens wanted to leave it that way. Others were reluctant to commit the huge sums of money that Pericles wanted. One of his strengths was his ability to persuade the citizens to follow his lead. It also helped that he enjoyed a reputation for complete honesty. It took all these powers to persuade his fellow citizens to undertake this massive and very expensive building project, which began in 447. Athens alone didn't have the money. Pericles—a man of unquestioned personal honesty—didn't have a problem dipping into the Delian League's treasury to help finance the project. Not surprisingly, the other league members weren't happy. A number of his fellow citizens shared the same feeling. They thought that Pericles wanted a monument to himself.

In the long view of history, Pericles' determination was worth the expenditure. With its gleaming buildings that contained more than 20,000 tons of marble, the Acropolis was soon regarded as one of the wonders of the ancient world. This high regard continues today. Every year uncounted thousands of tourists troop through the remains, which are impressive despite centuries of exposure to the weather, looting, and a disastrous explosion. It was Pericles' most lasting legacy.

At the same time, the annual civic theatrical competitions became even more important. Aeschylus was joined in the annual competitions by two other playwrights, Sophocles and Euripides. The comic playwright Aristophanes (air-uh-STOF-uh-neez) also began to claim his share of fans.

Athens had become a thriving center of intellectual activity. The notables included Herodotus, generally regarded as the first historian, who wrote a vivid description of the wars with the Persians and Spartans. Others were philosophers such as Pericles' old tutor Anaxagoras and a rising young teacher named Socrates.

The famous historian Thucydides (thoo-SID-ih-deez) summarizes what had happened: "What was in name a democracy became in actuality rule by the first man."[5] Yet Athens was by no means a dictatorship. Like any other Athenian politician, Pericles was always subject to the will of the people. He could be voted out of office at any time, or even ostracized. It is a tribute to his political skills that he managed to maintain his position as his city's leader for three decades.

At the peak of his power, Pericles did something that has ruined the careers of countless numbers of politicians. He became involved with a woman who had a dubious reputation.

The Acropolis

From the earliest days of Athens, the Acropolis was one of the city's most important features. Rising more than 100 feet above its surroundings, it first served as the city's place of safety as its sheer walls defied enemies who tried to capture it. Then it became the site of temples.

When Pericles convinced the Athenians to rebuild, he spared no expense, hiring the best architects and sculptors and buying the best possible materials. Its focal point was the Parthenon, which even today draws all eyes. It is more than 200 feet long, over 100 feet wide, and soars upward more than 60 feet. The sculptor Phidias (FID-ee-us) constructed two huge marble statues of Athena, the city's patron goddess. They were decorated in gold and ivory.

Propylaea

The Parthenon, while the most costly part of the project, wasn't the only attraction. The Propylaea made an impressive entryway. The site included two other temples, the Erectheum and the temple of Nike, the goddess of victory. All the buildings were brightly painted and included a number of sculptures.

Greece eventually became a part of the Roman Empire. When it adopted Christianity as its official religion, the Parthenon became a church. Zealous Christians defaced the sculptures because they honored pagan gods. Later, when the Turkish Ottoman Empire took over Greece, the Parthenon became a Muslim mosque. Late in the 17th century, the Turks were at war with the Venetians, and Athens became a battlefield. A Venetian shell detonated gunpowder the Turks had stored inside the Parthenon and largely demolished the magnificent building. It lay in ruins for decades.

Now partially rebuilt, it faces another enemy: polluting acid rain that eats away at the ancient marble, which has suffered more in the past few decades than in the twenty-five centuries since its construction. The Greek government, mindful of the importance of the Parthenon as a symbol of the country's past greatness and as an attraction for present-day tourists, has committed substantial resources toward its preservation.

This is a portrait of Aspasia, who caused a scandal when she and Pericles began living together. They showed much more affection toward each other than was customary at that time.

CHAPTER
FOUR

LOVE AND WAR

After his divorce, Pericles did not remarry. Apparently he turned over the responsibility of maintaining his house to a male slave, a somewhat unusual practice. He seemed content to live a quiet personal life, putting his energy into his increasingly important and busy public life.

Then around 450 B.C. he began a relationship with a woman named Aspasia, who was about twenty-five or thirty years younger than he was. She had been born in Miletus, which had made a recovery after its destruction by the Persians several decades earlier. When she came to Athens, she became a metic, a resident foreigner. While metics did not enjoy the full blessings of Athenian citizenship, they made valuable contributions to the city's prosperity.

Aspasia's contribution was to provide affection for Athenian men. As was customary, they rarely received affection at home. Athenian marriages tended to be based on practical considerations and were normally arranged by parents. Wives had three main responsibilities: to take care of the home, to produce children, and to stay out of trouble. As a result, they rarely went out in public.

Chapter FOUR

By the time she was in her late teens, Aspasia was among the city's most famous courtesans, as the women who performed her function were known. Even though she was very beautiful, men also respected her intelligence and enjoyed discussing important issues with her. Her hometown may have played a role in her intellectual development, since many famous philosophers came from Miletus.

It is not certain when she met Pericles, or how long it took for their relationship to develop. What is certain is that Pericles—by then in his mid to late forties—fell deeply in love with her. Soon they were living together. In every respect, he treated her as his wife. To the astonishment and disapproval of his fellow citizens, he would kiss her passionately and publicly when he left in the morning and when he returned in the evening.

It was entirely normal for an Athenian man to be associated with a courtesan. "What was by no means normal, but shocking and offensive to many, was to treat such a woman, and a foreigner too, as a wife: to lavish such affection on her as few Athenian wives enjoyed, involve her regularly in conversation with other men, and discuss important matters with her and treat her opinions with respect," writes Donald Kagan.[1]

Not surprisingly, Pericles and Aspasia created a scandal. Part of the problem was that while Pericles was highly respected, he was not especially loved. He was a somewhat cold person who largely kept to himself. Except for his passion toward Aspasia, he rarely allowed his feelings to come out. His one concession to vanity involved his head. He considered it somewhat misshapen, so he never allowed anyone to make sculptures of him unless he was wearing his helmet to cover the disfiguration.

As a result of his aloofness, he and Aspasia were subjected to merciless gossip. One of the most notorious accusations was that she wrote his speeches. This was especially humiliating in male-

This diorama shows the sculptor Phidias at work on the Frieze of the Parthenon. Elaborately carved and decorated, it depicts a religious festival and shows both gods and mortal beings.

dominated Athens. Eventually gossip became something much more serious. Pericles had always had political enemies. His importance to the city made it difficult to attack him head-on, so his enemies tried a somewhat indirect approach. They brought charges that included impiety against several people closely associated with him— Anaxagoras (his old teacher), Phidias (the sculptor of the great statue of Athena that dominated the Parthenon), and Aspasia herself. In a society as religiously oriented as Athens, these were serious matters. Anaxagoras and Phidias were punished. Only a direct appeal from Pericles himself in front of the jury trying Aspasia spared her. He broke down and cried.

But soon Pericles' problems with Aspasia were replaced by something far more serious. The long-simmering problems with Sparta were coming to a full boil. By then, most of the Greek city-states were allied with one or the other of the two rivals. It was ironic that Sparta,

The Spartan army (at left) appears poised to claim yet another victory, as its disciplined soldiers move forward in an attack formation.

which was ruled by two kings and a few other men, was able to present itself as the defender of freedom. Spartan propaganda successfully painted democratic Athens as an oppressor. There was a great deal of truth in the Spartan charges, as Athens was often ruthless in what it regarded as its own self-interest. Some of its so-called allies were being forced to support Athens.

Historian Norman Cantor explains, "Antagonism between the two sides finally led to Spartan demands that Athens grant concessions to Corinth [a Spartan ally]. Pericles persuaded the Athenian Assembly that compliance would only convince Sparta of Athens's weakness and that more demands would surely follow."[2]

His hard line carried the day. Athens refused the Spartan demands. When word reached Sparta in the summer of 431, the most potent army in Greece went on the march toward Athens. What became known as the Peloponnesian War (because Sparta was located in the Peloponnesian Peninsula of Greece) had begun. It would prove catastrophic for Athens and all of Greece.

Spartan Warfare

Most battles among Greek city-states took the form of clashes between heavily armored infantrymen known as hoplites. The troops would form long rows and columns called phalanxes (FAY-langk-ses) that were usually at least eight men deep. Each man held a large heavy shield in his left arm and a spear with a lethal iron tip in his right. The shields would overlap, lending strength to the lines.

According to writer Bruce Thornton, "Each line marched toward the other to the accompaniment of a flute, then ran the last few hundred yards to give more impetus to their spear thrusts, colliding in a horrible dusty din of clashing bronze and wood, splintering shields and spears, war cries, prayers, shouts of help and encouragement, and screams of agony."[3]

Inches away from their enemies, the men did anything—biting, kicking, gouging—to gain an advantage. Anyone who fell was doomed, from suffocation, being trampled, or being stabbed by sharp points on the butt end of the spears. The men in the rear of the phalanx would lean forward into the backs of those in front and push with their shields. The object was to push so hard that the opponents would crack, panic, throw down their shields and run away.

No one was better at hoplite warfare than Sparta. Spartan boys were taken away from their parents at the age of seven to live in barracks and begin military training. They were treated harshly by older boys to make them immune to pain and hardship as they grew up. Spartan warriors had almost no personal freedom. On the other hand, they didn't have to worry about earning a living. Thousands of slaves called Helots worked in the fields.

As Thornton continues, "All their time was spent developing few skills or talents other than the physical and psychological ones needed to stand unflinching in the line across from the gleaming bronze and bristling spears of the enemy, and then to endure the collision of bronze and iron."[4]

There was a common saying among Spartans: "Come back with your shield—or on it." That meant the only honorable options were victory or death. A Spartan who lost his shield would be suspected of running away. There was no place in Sparta for cowards.

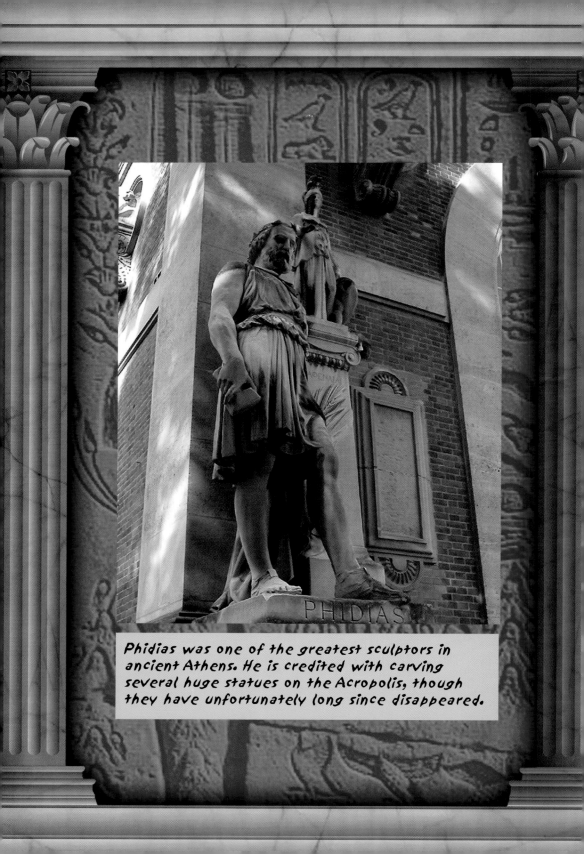

Phidias was one of the greatest sculptors in ancient Athens. He is credited with carving several huge statues on the Acropolis, though they have unfortunately long since disappeared.

CHAPTER
FIVE

THE GREEK TRAGEDY

In August 1914, many European soldiers marched off to war. Bands played, women threw flowers, and spirits were high. No one could forecast the bloody horror that became World War I, the millions of men who would be maimed or killed, or the massive changes in society and disillusionment that would result from the carnage.

The situation was similar in 431 B.C. as the Athenians made their preparations to resist the oncoming Spartans. Years earlier, Pericles had persuaded his fellow citizens to build the Long Walls, a series of formidable fortifications that linked the port city of Piraeus with Athens.

Pericles' plan was to allow the Spartans to invade the countryside around Athens, burning crops and farmhouses. The Athenians would be safe inside their protective walls. Because their navy controlled the seas, the vital overseas grain shipments could continue. At the same time, the navy could conduct a series of hit-and-run raids against the Spartans and their allies.

Pericles assumed that the war would be relatively short, and that it would end with few substantial changes. That had been the pattern of previous wars involving the Greek city-states. At first, events seemed to prove him correct. As predicted, the Spartans poured into the undefended countryside, destroying everything that lay in their path. But they couldn't get inside Athens. With the approach of winter, they went back home. The Athenians left the city and began the process of rebuilding.

During that period, Pericles delivered what has become famous as his Funeral Oration. Only a handful of Athenians had died—so far. Pericles knew there would be many more. In much the same manner that Abraham Lincoln used his Gettysburg Address to remind his listeners of the cause for which the Union soldiers had died, Pericles explained the meaning of Athenian democracy to the assembled mourners. Some of the language that Lincoln used is even similar to Pericles' phrasing two and a half millennia earlier.

There was no boasting in the speech. Pericles did not use it as an occasion to puff up his own importance. Rather, he stressed the importance of Athenian ideals. The citizens worked together for the common good, rather than for their own selfish ends. Because they were responsible for their own laws, they obeyed these laws because they wanted to, not because they were forced to.

"We will be admired by this and future generations," Pericles said. He praised the fallen warriors: They knew "that it meant resisting and dying rather than starving by submission, they fled disgrace in word but stood up to the deed with their lives."[1]

It is likely that many of the Founding Fathers of the United States, who learned about Greek history as part of their education, read the Funeral Oration, and that Pericles' words influenced their actions as they first declared independence from Great Britain and later wrote the U.S. Constitution.

The following spring, the campaign renewed. Again the Spartans ran roughshod through the countryside. Again the Athenians withdrew inside the Long Walls. They were safe from the invaders. The human invaders, that is. With the entire population cooped up in a small area, the conditions were perfect for another type of invader.

Nobody could see these new invaders. Nobody knew where they came from. Soon everybody knew about them. "They" were germs. They caused a horrible plague. Even today, no one knows which disease it was. That didn't make any difference to those who came down with it. More than 20 percent of the citizens died agonizing deaths, including both Xanthippus and Paralus, Pericles' sons. The survivors, dazed and angry, needed someone to blame. Pericles was a convenient target.

Over his objections, a delegation went to Sparta to seek peace. The Spartans, sensing the desperation of the Athenians, refused to negotiate. The Athenians then stripped Pericles of his generalship. Soon the plague lost its effects. The Athenians began to feel more confident and reelected Pericles. They also did him a favor. Aspasia had given him a son, also named Pericles, probably in 440. Under the terms of the law he had advocated earlier, the boy could not be considered an Athenian citizen. Grief-stricken after burying his grown sons, Pericles now tearfully asked the Athenians to give him special dispensation and grant his only surviving son the full rights of Athenian citizenship. They granted his wish. It was perhaps his final moment of happiness. Soon he contracted the disease that had killed so many of his fellow citizens. While he lived much longer than most victims, he couldn't fight off its effects forever. In the autumn of 429, he died.

Athens had just begun the greatest crisis in its existence since the Persian invasions. The life of its greatest leader had just ended. Somewhat surprisingly, it didn't seem to make much difference at first. The war settled into a series of relatively inconclusive engagements. With the plague over, life in Athens returned to normal. Theatrical contests returned. In 421 B.C.—a decade after hostilities had begun—the two sides even declared a truce.

Pericles delivers his famous Funeral Oration to the citizens of Athens. His words honored the first soldiers to die during the Peloponnesian War and reminded his listeners of the cause for which they were fighting.

It didn't last. Six years later the Athenians committed a large part of their army and fleet to an invasion of the Greek colony of Syracuse on the island of Sicily in an effort to expand their empire. Unfortunately, dissension and indecisive leadership doomed the effort. In 413, the Athenian fleet was trapped inside the harbor and destroyed. The Athenian army was crushed. The survivors were worked to death as slaves in Syracusan quarries. It was the worst defeat in the city's history.

Somehow the Athenians were able to keep going. But they were simply postponing the inevitable. In 406, Pericles—the son of the great man—was elected as general. He helped win a naval battle soon afterward. But hundreds of Athenians whose ships had been sunk died in a storm that sprang up following the battle. Pericles and the other generals were condemned to death because they weren't able to rescue the men.

His city was soon to suffer the same fate. With their supremacy on land assured, the Spartans had begun building their own navy. In 405, the new Spartan fleet surprised the remnants of the Athenian navy and won an overwhelming victory. It placed the Spartans firmly in control of the route by which the Athenians received most of their grain.

Faced with mass starvation, Athens surrendered the following year. The long agony was over. The city would never be the same.

The victorious Spartans forced the Athenians to pull down the Long Walls. They instituted a government of their own choosing. This new government hunted down and murdered many of the remaining democratic leaders.

Sparta itself was doomed. Supremely gifted in war, the city had become the one remaining superpower in Greece. But its leaders soon proved incapable of governing their new territories. The city-states resumed their ceaseless little wars. And like the Persians before them, the Spartans eventually proved that they weren't invincible either. They were defeated in 371 at the battle of Leuctra (LUKE-truh) by a group of city-states led by Thebes. Within a few years, Greece became vulnerable to the northern Greek kingdom of Macedonia, under the command of Philip II. Under Philip's son, Alexander the Great, the Macedonians subjugated the city-states and swept eastward into Persia. Within ten years, they had carved out a huge empire. But Alexander died unexpectedly at the age of thirty-three. His generals soon fell into bickering. The way was clear for yet another empire to arise. It would be Rome. Never again would Greece rise to its earlier levels of importance as a political entity.

Greek ideals were another story. They would flourish. It is significant that perhaps the most influential book in the Western world—the New Testament of the Bible—was written in Greek. Greeks also influenced medicine, mathematics, science, literature, drama, and many other fields. Thousands of commonly used English words are based on the Greek language.

Perhaps most important, the brief period from 507 to 404—through much of which Pericles lived and exerted a dominating influence—gave us democracy, the belief that every person has an equal voice in government.

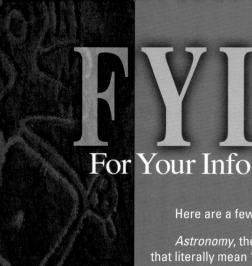

FYI
For Your Info

English Words from Greek

Literally thousands of English words trace their origins to Greek roots. These include our word *alphabet*, which is derived from combining *alpha* and *beta*, the first two letters of the Greek alphabet.

Here are a few other examples.

Astronomy, the study of outer space, comes from two Greek words that literally mean "star naming." *Astronauts*, the brave women and men who venture into space, are "star sailors." The symbol of the Houston Astros baseball team is, appropriately, a star.

When scientists began uncovering fossils of huge prehistoric creatures, for some they used Greek words meaning "terrifying lizards," from which we get *dinosaurs*. The most ferocious was the mighty *Tyrannosaurus rex*, the "tyrant king lizard." Others of these creatures could fly, so they were named *pterodactyls*, or "winged fingers."

Hippopotamuses, those lumbering water-loving mammals, are "river horses." *Chameleons*, which change their color to blend into their surroundings, are "dwarf lions." The Greeks also conceived of imaginary animals such as the *chimera* (kie-MAIR-uh), or "she-goat." This fearsome, fire-breathing creature had a lion's head, a goat's body, and a serpent's tail. Now the word means "illusion." The Greeks also gave us *dragon*, which means "serpent."

Trapeze originally meant "small table." Greek bankers in the time of Pericles conducted their business from small tables in bustling marketplaces. In modern Greece, a trapeza is a bank. Its English meaning comes from its shape: the bar, the two parallel ropes that support the bar, and the ceiling form a rectangle similar to a table.

When you hold a *kaleidoscope* to your eye and rotate it, you see constantly changing combinations of colorful shapes. The word's literal meaning is "beautiful seeing." A *telescope* is "far seeing," while a microscope is "tiny seeing."

Stadium comes from the length of a Greek footrace, about 200 yards. Spectators inside a Greek stadium could watch the *discus* throw, from a word meaning "flat." That same root gives us words such as *dish* and *desk*.

Chronology

All dates B.C.

493	Pericles is born in Athens
480	Escapes from Athens during Persian invasion
472	Serves as *choregos* for Aeschylus's play *The Persians*
463	Possible date of marriage
461	Assumes political leadership after Ephialtes is assassinated
457	Commands squadron of ships in conflict with Sparta and Thebes
454	Transfers Delian League treasury from the island of Delos to Athens
451	Passes citizenship law
450	Begins living with Aspasia
449	Signs peace treaty with Persia
448	Plans building project on Acropolis; construction begins the following year
440	Birth of son Pericles
431	Begins Peloponnesian War; gives funeral oration for first Athenian victims
430	Is removed from office
429	Is reinstated in office; dies in Athens from the plague

BIOGRAPHY FROM

ANCIENT CIVILIZATIONS

LEGENDS, FOLKLORE, AND STORIES OF ANCIENT WORLDS

Timeline in History

All dates B.C.

539	Persian emperor Cyrus II frees the Jews from their captivity in Babylon and allows them to return to Israel.
527	Athenian tyrant Peisistratus dies and is replaced by his sons, Hippias and Hipparchus.
525	The future playwright Aeschylus is born.
519	Xerxes I, a future Persian emperor, is born.
509	Rome expels its king and becomes a republic.
507	Under the leadership of Cleisthenes, Athens becomes the world's first democracy.
492	The Persians crush Miletus and decide that Athens will be their next target.
490	The Athenian victory at Marathon is the first defeat of Persian power.
484	Greek historian Herodotus is born.
480	An outnumbered Greek fleet under the leadership of Athenian general Themistocles defeats Persians at the battle of Salamis.
479	The Greek victory in the battle of Plataea ends the Persian threat.
478	The Delian League is formed under Athenian leadership.
470	The philosopher Socrates is born.
465	Xerxes is assassinated.
460	The "Father of Medicine," Hippocrates, is born; Conflict between Athens and Sparta begins.
458	Aeschylus's *Oresteia*, the most famous group of Greek tragic plays, premieres.
456	Aeschylus dies.
445	Conflict between Athens and Sparta ends.
431	The Peloponnesian War begins.
413	The Athenians suffer a crippling defeat at Syracuse on the island of Sicily.
404	The Peloponnesian War ends.
399	Socrates is sentenced to commit suicide by drinking hemlock.
371	Thebans victorious over Spartans at the battle of Leuctra.
356	Alexander the Great is born.
338	King Philip II of Macedon defeats a combined Greek army at Chaeronea.
146	Rome completes conquest of Greece at the battle of Corinth; Greece becomes a Roman province.

Chapter Notes

CHAPTER TWO   **A RISING STAR**

  1. Herodotus, *The Histories*, translated by Aubrey de Selincourt (New York: Penguin Books, 1972), p. 307.

  2. Donald Kagan, *Pericles of Athens and the Birth of Democracy* (New York: Macmillan, 1991), p. 25.

CHAPTER THREE   **BUILDING FOR THE AGES**

  1. Plutarch, *The Lives of the Noble Grecians and Romans, Volume 1*, trans. by John Dryden, edited and revised by Arthur Hugh Clough (New York: The Modern Library, 1992), p. 656.

  2. Donald Kagan, *Pericles of Athens and the Birth of Democracy* (New York: Macmillan, 1991), p. 43.

  3. Ibid., p. 45.

  4. Paul Cartledge, *The Greeks: Crucible of Civilization* (New York: TV Books, 2000), p. 104.

  5. Thucydides, *The Peloponnesian War*, translated by Donald Lattimore (Indianapolis: Hackett Publishing Company, 1998), p. 107.

CHAPTER FOUR   **LOVE AND WAR**

  1. Donald Kagan, *Pericles of Athens and the Birth of Democracy* (New York: Macmillan, 1991), pp. 182–83.

  2. Norman F. Cantor, *Antiquity: The Civilization of the Ancient World* (New York: HarperCollins, 2003), p. 114.

  3. Bruce Thornton, *Greek Ways: How the Greeks Created Western Civilization* (San Francisco: Encounter Books, 2000), p. 89.

  4. Ibid, p. 90.

CHAPTER FIVE   **THE GREEK TRAGEDY**

  1. Thucydides, *The Peloponnesian War*, translated by Donald Lattimore (Indianapolis: Hackett Publishing Company, 1998), pp. 94–95.

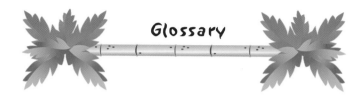

Glossary

betrothed	(bee-TROTHED)—person to whom one is engaged to be married.
epoch	(EH-pock)—a memorable period of time.
exiled	(EX-iled)—forced to live away from one's native land.
hoplite	(HOP-lite)—a heavily armored Greek soldier.
impiety	(im-PIE-uh-tee)—lacking proper respect for religious customs.
juggernaut	(JUH-ger-nawt)—a seemingly irresistible force.
lyre	(LIAR)—a stringed instrument, similar to a small harp, that was used to accompany songs and poetry readings.
ostracized	(AWS-truh-sized)—sent into temporary exile by means of a popular vote.
pragmatic	(prag-MA-tick)—relating to practical matters.
roughshod	(RUFF-shawd)—carried out with exceptional force.
scion	(SIE-uhn)—a descendent.
swath	(SWAWTH)—a long area in which everything is cut down.

BIOGRAPHY FROM ANCIENT CIVILIZATIONS

LEGENDS, FOLKLORE, AND STORIES OF ANCIENT WORLDS

For Further Reading

For Young Adults

Jones, John Ellis. *Ancient Greece*. New York: Warwick Press, 1983.

Nardo, Don. *The Age of Pericles* (World History Series). San Diego: Lucent Books, 1996.

———. *The Battle of Marathon*. San Diego: Lucent Books, 1996.

Robinson, Charles Alexander Jr. *Ancient Greece*. New York: Franklin Watts, 1984.

Walsh, Jill Paton. *Children of the Fox*. New York: Farrar, Straus and Giroux, 1978.

Warner, Rex. *Athens at War*. New York: E. P. Dutton, 1971.

Works Consulted

Bowra, C. M. *Periclean Athens*. New York: The Dial Press, 1971.

Cantor, Norman F. *Antiquity: The Civilization of the Ancient World*. New York: HarperCollins, 2003.

Cartledge, Paul. *The Greeks: Crucible of Civilization*. New York: TV Books, 2000.

Dersin, Denise (editor). *What Life Was Like at the Dawn of Democracy: Classical Athens 525–322 B.C.* Alexandria, Virginia: Time-Life Books, 1997.

Herodotus. *The Histories*. Translated by Aubrey de Selincourt. New York: Penguin Books, 1972.

Kagan, Donald. *Pericles of Athens and the Birth of Democracy*. New York: Macmillan, 1991.

Plutarch. *The Lives of the Noble Grecians and Romans, Volume 1*. Translated by John Dryden. Edited and revised by Arthur Hugh Clough. New York: The Modern Library, 1992.

Thornton, Bruce. *Greek Ways: How the Greeks Created Western Civilization*. San Francisco: Encounter Books, 2000.

Thucydides. *The Peloponnesian War*. Translated by Donald Lattimore. Indianapolis: Hackett Publishing Company, 1998.

On the Internet

"The Acropolis of Athens"
http://www.dragonridge.com/greece/ Acropolis.htm

"The Age of Pericles: Athens as Metropolis"
http://mars.acnet.wnec.edu/~grempel/courses/ wc1/lectures/08pericles.html

"Ancient Drama"
http://www.geocities.com/Broadway/Balcony/ 7634/ancient_drama.htm

Athens City Guide
http://www.athensguide.gr/pop/acropolis.html

Denault, Leigh T. "The Glory That Was Greece: Culture and History in Ancient Athens"
http://www.watson.org/~leigh/athens.html

"Greek Drama"
http://www.wsu.edu:8080/~dee/GREECE/ DRAMA.htm

The Greeks: Crucible of Civilization— "Pericles"
http://www.pbs.org/empires/thegreeks/htmlver/ characters/f_pericles.html

Plutarch. "Pericles, 'The Olympian' "
http://www.e-classics.com/pericles.htm

Index

Acropolis   22, 29
Aeschylus   19, 21, 28
Agariste (Pericles' mother)   15
Alcmaeonids   15, 16, 18
Alexander the Great   41
Anaxagoras   17, 18, 28, 33
Ariphron (Pericles' brother)   15
Aristophanes   28
Aspasia   30, 31, 32, 33, 39
Cimon   16, 23, 24, 25, 26
Cleisthenes   15
Damon   17–18
Darius the Great   10, 11
Delian League   24, 26, 28
Dionysus   19, 20, 21
Diorama   33
Ephialtes   24, 25, 26
Euripides   21, 28
Greaves (bronze)   8, 9
Herodotus   13, 16, 28
Homer   17, 18
Lincoln, Abraham   38
Long Walls   37, 38, 39
Louis, Spiridon   13
Leuctra, battle of   41
Marathon, Battle of   7–10, 15, 16
Miletus   7, 31, 32
Miltiades   16, 23
Olympics   13
Paralus (Pericles' son)   19, 20, 39
Parthenon   22, 27, 29

Pericles
    Becomes political leader   25–26
    Begins political career   23
    Birth of   15
    Builds on Acropolis   27-28
    Death of   39
    Delivers Funeral Oration   38
    Education of   17–18
    Father ostracized   17
    Funeral oration   38, 40
    Marriage of   19
    Outbreak of Peloponnesian War
        33–34, 40
    Outbreak of plague   39
    Relationship with Aspasia   32–33
    Sponsors *The Persians*   19
Pericles (Pericles' son)   39, 40
Pheidippides   8, 13
Phidias   29, 33, 36
Philip II of Macedonia   41
Propylaea   29
Salamis, Battle of   11–12, 17, 19
Socrates   28
Sophocles   21, 28
Spartans   8, 10, 23, 24–25, 28, 34, 35,
    37–40, 41
Themistocles   11, 19
Thespis   21
Thucydides   28
Xanthippus (Pericles' father)   16, 17
Xanthippus (Pericles' son)   19, 20, 39
Xerxes   10, 11, 12